HoW To MEDITATE

D0059407

HoW To
MEDITATE

*A step-by-step guide to the
art and science of meditation*

JOHN NOVAK

Cover photos: John Novak
Inside photos: George R. Beinhorn

Revised Edition (4th printing) 1992

Copyright © 1989 by John Novak
International Book Number 0-916124-55-X
Printed in the United States
10 9 8 7 6 5 4

Contents

Preface 7

Meditation 11

Getting Started 17

Section 1 — Relaxation

Relaxing the Body 25

    Deep Yogic Breath 26

    The Corpse Pose 28

    Diaphragmatic Breathing 30

    Proper Posture for Meditation 31

Relaxing the Mind 33

    Regular Breathing 38

    Alternate Breathing 39

Section 2 — Interiorization

Interiorization 45

    Watching the Breath 47

    Chanting 51

    Visualization 55

Section 3 — Expansion

Expansion 61

    Devotion 62

    Inner Communion 63

    Intuitive Answers to Problems 65

    Transition to Activity 67

The Basic Routine for Meditation 69

Section 4 — Application

Application 77

Relationships 77
Work 79
Health and Healing 80
The Energization Exercises 84
The Spinal Centers 92
Patanjali's Eightfold Path 98
Yama, Niyama — Right Behavior 100
Asana, Pranayama, Pratyahara — Interiorization 105
Dharana, Dhyana, Samadhi — Expansion 108
About the Author 113
Resources 115

Preface

Originally this book was written to accompany a "How to Meditate" class series I taught. The students wanted a simple guide which reviewed the details of the meditation techniques they were learning. Because the book was meant only to supplement a much larger body of oral material, it was purposely kept very brief and succinct.

Over the years there has been a growing demand for this kind of short, practical guide to the art and science of meditation. While there is much to be gained by brevity, there is also something inevitably lost. I urge readers of this book to expand their understanding of meditation, and the philosophy of life from which it sprang, through further study and, more importantly, daily practice.

The material covered here is based primarily on the teachings of Paramhansa Yogananda and his disciple Kriyananda, who is my teacher. Paramhansa Yogananda was one of the greatest yogis ever to teach in America. Coming to this country from India in 1920, he spent the next 32 years here writing many books and lessons, lecturing to hundreds of thousands of students, and training dedicated disciples. He took the deepest philosophy and the highest techniques of the ancient science of yoga and put them into a language and system uniquely suited to the modern Western mind. His book, *Autobiography of a Yogi,* is a spiritual classic which has inspired innumerable readers throughout the world and has been translated into dozens of languages.

Kriyananda became Yogananda's disciple in 1948 and lived with him until the great master's passing in 1952. Kriyananda has taught yoga and its related applications for over forty years and, at last count, has written nearly forty books on the subject, including *The Path, A Spiritual Autobiography,* which tells about his years with Paramhansa Yogananda. I cannot recommend highly enough the writings of these two great teachers. Their works are listed in the *Resources* section at the end of this book.

In 1968 Kriyananda founded the spiritual community Ananda Cooperative Village, which is a living laboratory for these teachings. Ananda, located in the foothills of the Sierra Nevada mountains of California, is commonly considered the most successful community of its kind in the world. It has over three hundred full-time residents, some seventy homes, its own school system, and many businesses. Ananda also includes four urban branch communities in the United States, a branch community near Assisi, Italy, and more than fifty meditation groups throughout the world.

I am a founding member of Ananda, and have lived and taught there since 1969. My wife and I serve, under Kriyananda, as the spiritual directors of Ananda. Over the last twenty years I have had the opportunity to teach, counsel, and form deep friendships with many hundreds of truth seekers. I have seen, first hand, the power of these teachings to transform lives.

I pray that this book can serve as a guide to this wonderful science. May your spiritual quest be filled with joy.

John (Jyotish) Novak

Meditation

Meditation is one of the most natural and yet most profoundly rewarding of all human activities. The great master of yoga, Paramhansa Yogananda, defined meditation as deep concentration on God or one of His aspects. Practiced on a daily basis it produces astonishing results on all levels of your being — physical, mental, emotional, and spiritual. It connects you with your own inner powers of vitality, clarity, and love. When done deeply, it also connects you with God and His infinite joy.

Meditation has three stages — relaxation, interiorization, and expansion. The process, stated simply, is:

1) Relax completely, both physically and mentally;

2) Interiorize the mind and concentrate it one-pointedly on your own higher self or some aspect of God; and

3) Expand your consciousness until your individual mind merges with the Infinite.

Although this process can be stated simply, the actual attainment of the deepest states requires dedication and discipline. Yet even a little practice of meditation will give immediate results. As it says in India's great scripture, the *Bhagavad Gita,* "Even a little practice of this inward religion will save one from dire fears and colossal sufferings."

There is an innate yearning in each of us to expand our awareness; to understand the nature of the universe; to know who and what we really are; to experience union with God. At a certain stage in this "eternal quest," as Paramhansa Yogananda called it, we are led inevitably to still the mind and practice meditation. Restless thoughts are a kind of mental "static" which must be silenced if we are to hear the whispers of our inner self.

The most profound perceptions about the nature of reality come through intuition rather than logic, from the superconscious rather than the conscious mind. When the body is completely relaxed, the five senses internalized, and the mind totally focused, a tremendous flow of energy becomes available. That intense energy lifts us into superconsciousness, where our inner powers of intuition are fully awake, and we become aware of personal and universal realities barely dreamed of before. But even a little internalization of the consciousness lifts us *toward* that state and benefits us on all levels.

Physiologically, meditation has been found, among other things, to reduce stress, strengthen the immune system, and help the body's healing processes. During meditation the breath and brain waves slow, blood pressure and metabolic rate decrease, and circulation and detoxification of the blood increase. A recent study of patients with coronary artery disease showed that a combination of meditation, *hatha yoga,* and a natural vegetarian diet could reverse the disease far better than the best traditional medical treatment presently available.

Mentally, meditation focuses and clarifies the mind better than any other activity. James J. Lynn, the most advanced disciple of Paramhansa Yogananda, was the founder and chief executive of one of the largest insurance companies in the country. He would arrive at his office late in the morning after several hours of meditation. When associates wondered how he could accomplish all his work with such a "relaxed" schedule, he responded that it was meditation that enabled him to do all his work. With his mind completely centered he would make decisions in a few moments that could otherwise have taken weeks.

While the physical and mental benefits of meditation are great, it is first and foremost a spiritual art. Its purpose, ultimately, is to lead us to perfection, to the realization that we are one with the Infinite. We come from God and are made in His image, and our hearts are restless until we again achieve unity (*yoga* in Sanskrit) with Him. Like lotuses opening to the sun, we are compelled by our own higher nature, the spark of God within, to move into the light of inner communion with Him. Meditation is the direct pathway to this divine state.

In recent years meditation has become commonly accepted and widely practiced in the West. It is now taught in churches, recommended by physicians, and widely practiced by athletes. There are meditation chapels in airports, hospitals, and even in Congress. It has been estimated that more than two million people in America practice meditation regularly.

It is an ancient art, going back in time to a period long before historical records were kept. Stone seals showing people seated in various yoga postures have been found in the Indus Valley of India and dated by archaeologists to at least 5000 B.C. Yet for all those millenniums, meditation has continued as a living, vital science.

Every religion has some branch (often somewhat secret) that seeks mystical union, and a form of meditation to achieve that end. And every age has examples of great men and women who have achieved Self-realization, or union with the Divine. In the East both a science and a tradition of meditation developed. Over the centuries great sages and teachers discovered truths and techniques which they passed on to their disciples, who in turn passed it on to their followers. Thus developed an unbroken tradition of thousands of years. That which proved true and lasting survived, while that which was tainted with ignorance fell by the wayside. Moreover, a society developed in the East which looked to these great ones for examples of how to live. Children still grow up in India being taught through stories and examples from the lives of enlightened souls such as Rama and Krishna, two great saints of ancient India. It has been said that the greatness of a culture can be judged by its heroes. In the East, and particularly in India, the greatest heroes have been those with the highest spiritual attainments.

In the West, however, there has been no living tradition of meditation. Great saints there have certainly been, but they have tended to stand out as unique individuals who had to discover the pathway to the Infinite with little or no help. Moreover, they knew no techniques to channel the enormous inner energy awakened by their intense devotion. Without teachers to guide them, or techniques to help them, their lives often lacked any semblance of balance and were commonly beset with great physical suffering. And in a society which didn't understand, nor necessarily respect, sanctity, many had to face the opposition of their families and even their spiritual "superiors."

Our heroes in the West have tended to be more warlike than Godlike. Mahatma Gandhi was once asked what he thought of Western civilization. His wry but perfectly understandable reply was, "I think it would be a good idea." Finally, with the influx of teachings from India, the tradition and benefits of meditation are being introduced to the West. The practice of meditation has tremendous potential for enriching both our individual lives and our society. The historian Arnold Toynbee has called the introduction of the Eastern traditions into the West the most important influence in the twentieth century.

Getting Started

Meditation is a simple process which can be done any time and anywhere you can interiorize your mind. It is not based on dogma, faith, or ritual but is concerned, like science, with experimentation and experience. Just as science seeks to uncover the secrets of nature, meditation seeks to discover truths about the nature of consciousness. Its tools, rather than microscopes and oscilloscopes, are concentration and intuition. While nothing is needed for meditation except a willing and inquiring mind, there are a number of things that can be done to make the search easier. The following are helpful aids.

Set Aside a Special Area for Meditation

It is very helpful to have an area that is used only for meditation. It will help reinforce a meditative mood and, over time, will become filled with meditation "vibrations." A small room or closet is ideal as long as it can be well ventilated. If you don't have enough space for a whole room, then set aside a small area in your bedroom or some other room that can be kept just for meditation. Your area can be kept very simple — all you really need is a small cushion or a chair to sit on.

You may also want to set up a small altar with a picture or pictures of those great souls who particularly inspire you. Many people also like to have a small candle for evening meditations and perhaps an incense burner. Your altar can be elaborate or simple according to your own tastes. A pure heart is, in any case, the true altar.

Cooperate with Natural Forces

There are certain natural forces which can either help or oppose your efforts. Magnetic forces in the earth tend to pull one's energy down. Certain natural fibers serve as an insulation against these forces just as a rubber coating insulates an electrical wire. Traditionally, yogis sat on a tiger or deer skin, but it works nearly as well to cover your meditation seat with a woolen blanket, a silk cloth, or both.

Especially good times to meditate are dawn, dusk, noon, and midnight. At these times, the gravitational pull of the sun works in harmony with the natural polarity of the body. It is somewhat easier to meditate at night or early in the morning while others are asleep. Thoughts have power, and the restless thoughts of people around you will have a subtle tendency to make your meditations more restless.

Develop Good Habits

Good habits will be *the major force* in determining whether or not you benefit from the science of meditation. A bold statement, perhaps, but a true one. Good intentions and bursts of enthusiastic devotion will dissipate unless they become translated into daily habits.

The first thing you need to do is settle on *when* it is convenient to do your meditations. In choosing a time for meditation, regularity is the most important factor, so set a time when you can be consistent. Meditate every day. Even if you meditate only five or ten minutes at a time, at least start! Better yet, try to meditate fifteen to twenty minutes twice a day in the beginning and then increase the time gradually; but don't go beyond your capacity to enjoy each meditation. Depth of meditation is more important than the length of time spent. As you progress you will find that you naturally want to meditate longer. The more you meditate, the more you will want to meditate! Once you have chosen a time for your meditations, stick with it until a strong habit has time to form.

For most people, the best times are just after rising in the morning and just before bed at night. These times are the least likely to have scheduling conflicts, and it is easiest to re-program the subconscious mind, where habits are rooted, just after or before sleep. Many people also like to meditate before lunch or after work, before eating dinner. Wait at least a half hour after eating — up to three hours after a heavy meal — so there will not be competition for energy between digestion and meditation.

A very helpful means of increasing the length and depth of your meditations is to have at least one long meditation each week. Your long meditation should be about three times as long as your normal ones. If you are normally meditating for twenty minutes at a sitting, try, once a week, to meditate for an hour. Not only will you find that you can go deeper in the long meditation, but your usual twenty minutes will soon begin to seem short.

Group meditation is also very helpful. If possible, try to find a group of people who meditate regularly. The encouragement of others who have been meditating longer than you is a very powerful spiritual force. In the Indian scriptures it says that *satsang* (the company of other truth seekers) is the most important aid on the spiritual path after the grace of the guru.

Let us now address the three stages of meditation: relaxation, interiorization, and expansion.

Relaxation

Relaxation

The first stage in meditation is relaxation. To a great extent the chronic tension and restlessness of both body and mind is simply a result of habit. We are used to moving and tensing, to planning and worrying. Gradually the habit of restlessness becomes so deeply entrenched that it feels abnormal to allow the body to relax and the mind to become quiet.

As one sits to meditate it is very important to make a strong mental resolution to put aside all preoccupations with this world. Be determined to withdraw from all worldly involvement for a little while. Your problems and worries will still be there when you return. Christ said it beautifully: "But seek ye first the kingdom of God, and His righteousness; and all these things shall be added unto you. Take therefore no thought for the morrow: for the morrow shall take thought for the things of itself. Sufficient unto the day is the evil thereof." (Matthew 6:33,34)

Relaxing the Body

Start by relaxing the body. Learning to relax at will has benefits that extend beyond meditation to every aspect of life. It is very helpful to do a couple of simple relaxation techniques before actually starting your meditation. Here are two simple yoga postures which will relax the body and prepare you for meditation.

Deep Yogic Breath

Begin by standing upright, arms at the sides. Relax the body and center your consciousness in the spine. Become aware of your breath and be sure you are breathing deeply from the diaphragm.

Now slowly bend over from the waist, keeping the legs and spine straight. Exhale slowly but completely as you bend forward, allowing your body to come down as far as is comfortable. Pause for a few seconds in this position. Now inhale slowly as you raise the torso, expanding first the diaphragm, then the sides of the rib cage, and finally the upper part of the chest. As the inhalation proceeds and your body slowly comes upright, draw the hands up along the sides of the body, elbows extended outward. With the incoming breath, feel that you are drawing not only air, but also energy and life-force into every cell of the body and brain. Continue inhaling and raising the trunk and arms until you finally stretch the hands high above the head. At this point you should have inhaled as completely as possible. Hold this position for a few seconds. Now slowly exhale and relax into the original standing position with the arms at the sides. Repeat this three or four times.

Deep Yogic Breath

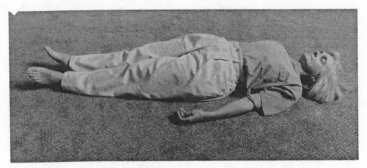

The Corpse Pose

The Corpse Pose (Savasana)

This posture is called the corpse pose because it helps withdraw all tension from the muscles. It is both the simplest and yet one of the most difficult of all the yoga postures. Physically it is extremely easy — the difficulty is that to practice it to perfection one must relax totally, not an easy thing for most people.

Lie flat on your back with your legs outstretched and your arms along the sides of your body. The body should be properly aligned, with the head, neck, trunk, and legs in a straight line. It is best to have the palms turned upward to help to induce a feeling of greater receptivity.

After assuming this position, begin a systematic relaxation of the whole body. Start by ridding the body of unconscious tension. This can be done by first tensing the body to increase the tension and then relaxing. There is a special "double breath" which helps oxygenate the system and remove toxins. It is done by inhaling through the nose with a short inhalation followed immediately by a longer one, in a huh/huuuuhh rhythm. Exhale through both the nose and mouth in the same huh/huuuuhh way. Inhale deeply with a double breath, tense the whole body until it vibrates, then throw the breath out in a double exhalation and relax. Do this three to six times, trying to relax your whole body after each round.

Now, consciously relax the various body parts. Start with the feet. It may help to think of the area being relaxed as becoming filled with space and growing very light, or conversely, so relaxed that it is extremely heavy and impossible to move. Gradually work your way up the body relaxing successively the calves, knees (especially behind the knees — a common area of subconscious tension), thighs, hips, abdomen (another common trouble spot), hands, forearms, upper arms, chest, neck, and face. As you get to the head, be sure to relax the jaw and tongue, the area around the eyes, and the forehead.

When you have relaxed the whole body, continue to lie still, feeling that you are floating on a warm sea with your breathing keeping rhythm with the rise and fall of the waves. Gradually, as you become even more relaxed both physically and mentally, feel that you are dissolving into the sea, becoming one with it and with all life. Try to hold on to this relaxed, expanded state for as long as possible. When it feels right to do so, gradually let your consciousness return to the body. Sit up slowly, staying as relaxed as possible, and go directly to your meditation.

Diaphragmatic Breathing

The deep relaxation of the corpse pose can also help you learn to breathe properly. Proper breathing starts with the diaphragm, a dome shaped sheet of muscle dividing the abdomen from the chest cavity. As this muscle contracts, it pushes down into the abdominal cavity, creating a space above it causing the lungs to expand and draw in a breath. A secondary expansion of the lungs is produced by expanding the rib cage and the chest. Deep, diaphragmatic breathing oxygenates and energizes the whole system. Unfortunately, few of us breathe properly. Women, especially, are prone to shallow breathing because the cultural bias toward a thin waist leads to a habit of unconsciously constricting the abdomen.

A perfect time to practice diaphragmatic breathing is during the corpse pose, when you are already deeply relaxed. As you breathe, allow the relaxed abdomen to expand gently upward with the inhalation and downward with the exhalation. In the beginning you may want to exaggerate this movement in order to help retrain yourself. After finishing the corpse pose, stand upright for a few minutes, and continue to practice diaphragmatic breathing.

Proper breathing also depends on proper posture. If you slump, it compresses the abdomen so the diaphragm doesn't have space to expand. Train yourself to stand and sit with the chest up, the shoulders slightly back, and the spine straight. This position not only helps you breathe properly but also allows you to relax more completely when you meditate.

A straight spine is important for spiritual reasons also. Learn to live more "in the spine," centered in the inner self rather than reacting constantly to the events of the world. Many of the most advanced techniques in yoga work with energies in the subtle, or *astral* spine. A tremendous storehouse of energy, the *Kundalini* power, rises deep in the subtle spine as enlightenment takes place. In India there is even a special order of swamis, called *Danda Swamis*, who carry a bamboo staff to remind themselves to always keep the spine straight.

Proper Posture for Meditation

In order to be able to relax the body sufficiently for meditation, proper posture is very important. And yet, there is nothing complicated about it. Simply sit upright with the spine erect and the body relaxed. The chest should be up, the shoulders slightly back, and the chin parallel to the floor. Imagine yourself as a marionette with a string pulling you upright from the top of the skull, allowing everything to fall into place. This position allows the spine to bear the weight of the torso. You can sit either in a straight-backed chair or on the floor in any comfortable cross-legged pose. If you use a chair, sit forward so nothing presses against your back. Place the hands, palms upright, at the junction of the thighs and abdomen to help keep the spine erect and the chest open. Your feet should rest flat on the floor. If you sit in a cross-legged position, you will probably find a cushion under the buttocks helpful. As mentioned earlier, it is helpful to cover your meditation seat with a woolen blanket or a silk cloth.

As you sit to meditate, first be sure the body is relaxed. If you have just finished the corpse pose, a quick mental check to see that you are still relaxed will be sufficient. If you have not yet relaxed the body, you should do so as soon as you begin. Follow the same routine as in the corpse pose. First inhale with a double breath, tense the whole body until it vibrates, then throw the breath out with a double breath. Do this three to six times. Then, starting with the feet and working your way up the body to the head, consciously relax every body part. When you are completely relaxed physically, it is time to relax mentally.

Cross-legged Posture for Meditation

Relaxing the Mind

Just as it is necessary to release the tensions in the muscles, it is also essential to release the tensions in the mind. Usually, mental tension is caused by preoccupations about the past or desires for the future. If we would live

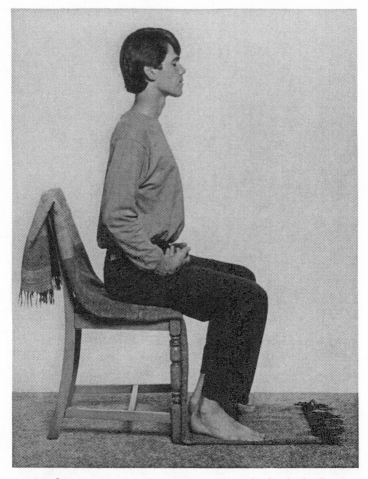

Meditation Posture Sitting on a Straight-backed Chair

completely in the here and now, it would be very easy to stay relaxed and happy. Meditation helps bring us into this state, but we must relax, at least partially, before we can begin to meditate effectively.

One of the most effective ways of relaxing the mind is to control the breathing. From ancient times, yogis have recognized that there is a direct link between the breath and the mind. In fact, the science of controlling the mind through breathing techniques, called *pranayama,* is one of India's great gifts to the world.

The word *prana* has three meanings — energy, life, and breath. *Prana* is used, first of all, to describe the universal energy which infuses and vitalizes all matter. Secondly, it means the presence of that energy in all living forms and, in this context, is used to refer to life itself. Yogananda called this aspect of *prana* "life-force," and explained that every particle of life-force possesses an inherent intelligence enabling it to carry out the life-sustaining processes.

Finally, and very importantly to the science of yoga, *prana* is also used to refer to the breath. There is a movement of *prana* in the subtle body which accompanies the physical breath. *Prana* flows up and down in the subtle spine in tandem with the inhalation and exhalation of air. Traditional *pranayama* (*prana* = energy and *yama* = control) techniques involve breathing exercises. Since our breath and the flow of *prana* are linked together, we can, by controlling the easily felt breath, indirectly control the much more subtle *prana*.

A direct feedback cycle also exists between the flow of breath/*prana* and the ability to concentrate the mind. A nervous or excited mental state is always accompanied by ragged breathing, and vice versa. You will notice that when you have a task requiring concentration, such as threading a needle, you automatically tend to slow or even hold your breath. Moods, too, are closely related to the flow of the breath. The next time you are in a negative mood, try breathing your way out of it using the deep yogic breath or one of the simple exercises below. You can use this technique even in times of great stress.

Mike, a friend and fellow disciple of ours, was in charge of training new recruits for the San Francisco Police. One technique he taught new rookies was to take control of their own breathing before trying to take control of a tense situation. "Take slow controlled breaths," he told them, "in order to keep yourselves calm and focused." He illustrated the importance of self-control through breath control with this true story:

One time, during a drug raid, Mike was chasing a man up a stairway in a darkened building. As he got to the top of the stairs he turned down a narrow hallway, to find the suspect pointing a shotgun at his chest. The man was obviously "high" on something and Mike knew that one false move on his part could be fatal. Holding the man's eyes with his own, he immediately started deep breathing, and mentally affirmed, "Be calm, be calm." After a minute or so he slowly held out his hand and asked the man to give him the gun. The man's shoulders finally slumped as the tension went out of him, and he surrendered without violence.

In the Olympic biathlon the participants must combine the extreme outward effort needed for cross-country skiing with the fine concentration needed to hit a target with a rifle shot. A few years ago the sport was transformed when the power of breath control was discovered. Now, as they race the last few hundred yards toward the target sites, all world-class participants use special controlled breathing techniques which slow the heart and concentrate the mind.

Most of us won't have our mental control tested under such extreme conditions, but our meditations can definitely benefit from the powerful connection that exists between breath control and mind control. Here are a couple of simple breathing techniques to relax the mind. The first one, "regular breathing," should be used at the beginning of every meditation.

Regular Breathing

As soon as you have relaxed the various body parts, do this technique to relax the mind: Inhale slowly, counting to twelve. Hold the breath for the same number of counts while concentrating at the point between the eyebrows. Then, slowly exhale for the same twelve count. This is one round of "regular breathing." Do six to nine rounds as you start to meditate. You can increase the count to 16:16:16, or decrease the number of counts to 8:8:8, according to your capacity, but be sure that the three phases — inhalation, holding, and exhalation — are all equal. Generally speaking, a slower rhythm is better, providing you are comfortable and don't get out of breath. Especially in the later rounds, you may want to increase the number of counts.

Concentrate completely on the breath, feeling that it is flowing in and out like the tide. As you exhale feel that you are letting go of all restless or negative thoughts. When you inhale feel that you are filling yourself not only with air but also with calm vitality. If you find that your mind has wandered, immediately bring it back to concentrating on the breath. Focus on the breath itself rather than the breathing process. The first few minutes of meditation are extremely important since they set the tone for the whole period. Determine, starting with the first breath of regular breathing, to stay inwardly focused.

Alternate Breathing

There is another simple breathing exercise or *pranayam,* called alternate breathing, that you will find helpful. This is similar to regular breathing, except the breath is inhaled through one nostril and exhaled through the other. Close the right nostril with the thumb of the right hand and inhale through the left nostril for a count of twelve. During the retention phase, gently squeeze the nostrils shut, using the thumb for one nostril and the ring and little fingers for the other. Hold the breath in this manner, concentrating deeply at the spiritual eye for twelve counts. Then, keeping the left nostril closed with the ring and little fingers, exhale through the right nostril. In *hatha yoga* there are names given for each phase: *purak* for inhalation, *rechak* for exhalation, and *kumbhak* for retention.

As in regular breathing, you can vary the number of counts according to what is comfortable, but keep the same count for all phases. This exercise is "cooling" to the nervous system, helping to calm the mind, because it works in harmony with the natural flows of magnetic energy in the body. Energy moves up the left side of the subtle spine as we inhale and down on the right as we exhale.

You may want to experiment by doing some variations of this technique. One variation is to do one round as described above and then the next round inhaling through the right nostril and exhaling through the left. This reverses the natural flow and gives an entirely different feeling, which many find heating or energizing to the nervous system.

Especially good for concentration is a variation in which the inhalation and exhalation are the normal twelve counts each, but the breath is held for a longer period of time, up to 25 or more counts, during the retention phase. Concentrate with great determination at the point between the eyebrows (also called the spiritual eye or the Christ center) while you are holding your breath.

These simple techniques are more important than you might think. People can meditate for many months or even years with meager results simply because they have ignored the basics, thinking that such elementary practices are only for the merest beginner. Restlessness, especially mental restlessness, is the main block to deeper meditation, and these basic breathing exercises are extremely effective in stilling the thoughts. For one thing, they require concentration, which breaks the momentum of mental restlessness. But more importantly, these techniques work with subtle energies little understood in the West.

"Our thoughts," Yogananda said, "are universally, not individually rooted." The astounding ramifications of this statement transform the present-day model of the thinking process. Instead of creating our own thoughts, we draw them from a universal pool of consciousness much as a radio receives a program. As we change the magnetism of our consciousness, we change the "program" we receive. Mental restlessness is like static which prevents the program from being heard clearly. Our first, and ultimately only job in meditation is to rid the mind of the static created by thoughts and desires. As soon as we can do this, we will see that our reality is not the ego (the receiver), but God, the Creator. The reason that meditation is so important to our spiritual search is that it is the only activity devoted specifically to totally calming the mind and ridding it of the whirlpools (or static) of egoic consciousness.

Once the body and mind have been relaxed, we are ready to proceed to the second stage of meditation: interiorization through concentration. Only after we have first interiorized all our energies can we proceed to the final stage of meditation: expansion of consciousness.

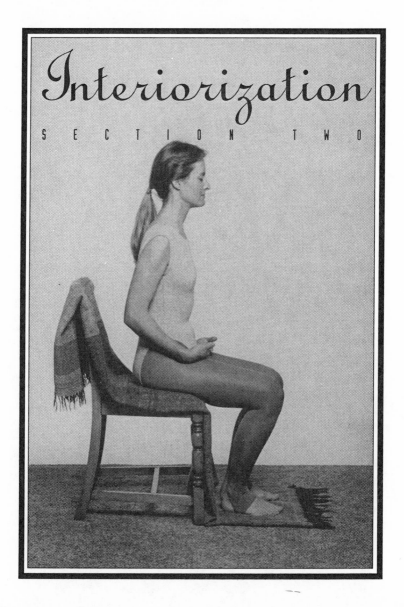

Interiorization

Interiorization

The next stage of meditation is the interiorization and concentration of energy as it manifests on physical, mental, and more subtle planes. In his book *Affirmations for Self-Healing,* J. Donald Walters (Kriyananda) writes:

> Concentration is the secret of success in every undertaking. Without concentration, thoughts, energy, inspiration, purpose — all one's inner forces — become scattered. Concentration is the calm focus of one's full attention on the purpose at hand. Concentration means more than mental effort: It means channeling your heart's feelings, your faith, and your deep aspirations into whatever you are doing. In that way, even the little things in life can become rich with meaning.

> Concentration should not involve mental strain. When you really want something, it is difficult *not* to think about it! Concentrate *with interest* on whatever you do, and you will find yourself absorbed in it.

While concentration is an ingredient for success in any area, it is absolutely essential for meditation. Meditation cannot exist without deep concentration. A special type of concentration is required for meditation — a focusing of the mind on inward realities rather than external objects. When we are engaged in activities our thoughts are normally focused on the object of our attention: a person, a book, the eye of a needle. But in order to carry on our inner search we need to withdraw our attention from the things of the world.

In meditation all of our scattered forces must be brought to a single point of concentration at the spiritual eye. Located in the frontal part of the brain at the point between the eyebrows, this is the center of will and intuition and the seat of superconsciousness or total awareness. Enlightenment takes place when all energy (or *prana*) — physical, mental, or subtle — can be focused at this point.

Relaxing the body as a preparation to meditation helps to free up energy being wasted as tension in the muscles, allowing us to use it to produce greater awareness. In deep meditation energy is withdrawn even from the internal bodily functions. In the deepest states, a yogi's heart and breath will stop. At that time enormous stores of energy can be concentrated at the spiritual eye.

Sleep is an unconscious way of withdrawing energy from the body and senses and refocusing it in the brain, and sleep is refreshing primarily due to this interiorization of energy. As far as the withdrawal of energy is concerned, sleep and meditation are similar. But meditation requires that we lift our awareness into superconsciousness, while in sleep it is allowed to slip into subconsciousness. If we didn't lose consciousness during sleep we could make very rapid spiritual progress. Paramhansa Yogananda humorously referred to sleep as "counterfeit *samadhi.*"

Mental energy in the form of restless thoughts also needs to be withdrawn and concentrated. When we no longer have an outward object to focus on, our thoughts usually become scattered. We tend to think about the past, worry and plan for the future, or daydream. These restless thoughts are the biggest block to meditation, but through strong determination and concentration we can overcome them.

The breathing techniques we have already learned will start the process of concentration. But yogis have developed more powerful techniques to help us internalize and concentrate mental energy. The three most powerful techniques are watching the breath, chanting (or repeating a *mantra* or prayer), and visualization.

Watching the Breath

Although simple to practice, this is one of the central and most important techniques of yoga. Watching the breath is extremely powerful because it works scientifically to calm the breath-*prana*-mind cycle. By concentrating intently on the breath and becoming a simple observer of the breathing process, we quickly calm the breath, redirect the flow of *prana* to the spiritual eye, and concentrate the mind.

1) The technique of watching the breath should be done immediately following the preparatory techniques, when you are already relaxed and focused. Begin by exhaling completely. As the next breath flows in, mentally watch it as if you were observing the flow of a tide. Be very aware of the breath, but make no attempt to control it in any way. Simply observe its natural flow. Try to feel the breath as it passes in and out of the nostrils. If you are unable to feel the breath in the nostrils, focus for a short time on the breathing process itself, the movement of the chest and lungs, and then transfer your awareness back to the breath in the nostrils.

2) To help deepen your concentration mentally repeat a simple word formula such as "Amen" in tandem with the breath. As you inhale silently say "A," and as you exhale silently repeat "men." Or you could say "I am" while inhaling and "He" while exhaling. Or simply count "one" with the incoming breath and "two" while exhaling. In India they silently repeat "*hong*" with the incoming breath and "*sau*" with the exhalation. This is a special *mantra* or word formula which is especially effective in calming the flow of *prana* in the spine. It is also helpful to move the index finger of the right hand slightly toward the palm on the inhalation and slightly away on the exhalation. If the mind wanders, immediately bring it back to concentrating on the technique.

3) As the breath becomes calmer, gradually become aware of it as it passes higher and higher in the nostrils until you are feeling it high up in the nasal cavity. Now you can transfer your point of concentration from the breath to the point between the eyebrows. This, according to the teachings of yoga, is the center of will in the body. It is the will that directs the flow of *prana,* and by concentrating here you engage a *pranic* switch in the task of interiorizing the energy. Continue to mentally observe the breath, and to silently chant your word formula, still making no effort to control either the rhythm or depth of your breathing.

4) The key to success with this technique is to deepen your concentration at the spiritual eye until you no longer think of *anything* except the rhythmic flow of the breath. As the mind becomes very focused and calm you will find your need for breath diminishing. Enjoy the spaces between breaths, keeping your mind very still and allowing the pauses to lengthen naturally. A cycle of increasing interiorization is set into motion through this technique. As the breath (and the flow of life-force) begins to calm down, the mind is naturally able to concentrate more deeply. Deeper concentration brings about an even greater calming of the *prana*/breath, allowing yet deeper focusing of the mind, and so on. The final stage of this cycle is the complete withdrawal of life current from the body and senses and the total concentration of the mind.

As the *prana* becomes completely focused at the spiritual eye, the body's need for oxygen ceases and the breath stops. At first this may be a somewhat odd and even frightening experience, but it is the doorway to the deepest states of meditation. In fact, Paramhansa Yogananda defined a "master" as one who is able to stop his breath at will.

5) End your practice of this technique by taking a deep breath and exhaling three times. Then concentrate very deeply at the spiritual eye, trying to hold your mind completely still. With the mind deeply concentrated and interiorized you can go on to the other parts of your meditation, such as concentrating on the light of the spiritual eye, listening to inner sounds, or feeling the deep love, peace, and joy brought by meditation.

Normally the technique of watching the breath should take up about a quarter of your meditation. However, you may want to practice it for a longer period at first or when you are feeling especially inspired. Yogananda, as a young man, would practice this technique for eight hours at a stretch! He suggested that those who want to become a master in this life practice it for two hours every day. How long should you practice it in any given meditation? Be guided by your own feeling of enjoyment and your ability to maintain your concentration. But remember, it is an extremely important technique designed to accomplish an absolutely essential purpose: total concentration leading to breathlessness. Without concentration, any time spent supposedly meditating is largely wasted.

6) Watching the breath is different from most other meditation techniques in that it can be practiced at any time when your concentration isn't needed for outward activities. It is greatly calming when you are nervous. Try practicing it the next time you're sitting in the dentist's office or before you have to do an unpleasant task. Once, as an experiment, I did a few rounds during a very tense scene in a movie. Within seconds all sense of anxiety had vanished!

Here are two other methods of achieving a state of deep concentration. The first, chanting, works with the verbalizing function of the mind while the other, visualization, engages yet another facet of the consciousness.

Chanting

Paramhansa Yogananda often said, "Chanting is half the battle." Chanting is one of the best ways to awaken spiritual fervor. We will make little progress on the spiritual path until we can direct the natural love of the heart toward God. Chanting also helps direct and focus the mind.

It is extremely difficult to go beyond the tendency to verbalize thoughts. Even when the mind is very calm, this habit tries to reassert itself. Rather than simply repress a normal mental function, we can use it to bring us to a deeper state of concentration and interiorization. This is done by first spiritualizing the words occurring in the mind and then concentrating one-pointedly on them.

A chant is a simple word formula, often an affirmation or prayer, such as "I want only Thee, Lord," set to music. Most chants are of a devotional nature and help awaken energy in the heart center and direct it toward a spiritual goal. Sometimes chants are in Sanskrit because of inherent power in the sounds themselves. More usually, however, the words are in English. By repeating them over and over we focus the mind, open the heart, and re-program the subconscious.

Start your meditations with a chant or two, first sung out loud and then silently. At first, sing vigorously in order to awaken energy. Gradually, however, focus the energy ever more inwardly. Eventually try to go beyond the words into the *vibration* being expressed. A very simple and beautiful chant, written by Kriyananda and sung often at Ananda, is *I Want Only Thee, Lord.* The words and music go like this:

I want on-ly Thee, Lord,   Thee,— on-ly Thee,

I want on-ly Thee, Lord,   Thee,— on-ly Thee.

I want on-ly Thee, Lord,   Thee, on-ly Thee,—

I want on-ly Thee, Lord,   Thee, on-ly Thee.

© 1986 by Donald Walters.

Start by singing the words out loud. After a few repetitions, chant the words more quietly and then silently, but with ever deepening concentration. Allow the words to be a means of devotionally communicating directly with the Lord. Yearn for Him! Ask Him, with all the intensity of heart and soul, to come to you! Let the words become secondary to your inward love and yearning until finally you can pass beyond words altogether, and speak to God with only the voice of your heart's devotion. It is in this charged atmosphere that He will come to you.

Chants can also be done later in your meditation, after you are deeply concentrated. Each chant emphasizes a slightly different facet of the multi-hued relationship with the Infinite. A favorite chant of Yogananda's, *Door of My Heart,* is very good for increasing one's devotion. The words are:

> *Door of my heart, open wide I keep for Thee. (repeat)*
> *Wilt Thou come, wilt Thou come? Just for once, come to me? (repeat)*
> *Will my days fly away without seeing Thee, my Lord? (repeat)*
> *Night and day, night and day, I look for Thee night and day. (repeat)*

Chanting is also an excellent way to stay connected to God throughout the day. By mentally singing as you go about work or stand in line at the supermarket, you can transform the most mundane task into a spiritual experience. The Indian term for repetitive chanting or prayer is *japa,* and it is one of the most widely practiced ways of communing with the Lord.

Playing a chanting tape as background music can change the whole vibration of your environment and is an excellent way to keep your mind uplifted. Music, because of its power to reach into the subconscious mind, is a much more important factor in influencing our moods than we realize. The environment we create around us has a tremendous effect on us. In fact, Yogananda often used to say, "Environment is stronger than will power." By creating, whenever possible, a spiritualized or uplifting environment, we keep our minds uplifted so that the "programs" we receive from the Infinite are elevating. In the *Resources* section at the end of the book we have listed several chanting tapes and books.

Visualization

This is another powerful way to focus the mind for meditation. Visualization bypasses the verbalizing areas of the brain and therefore helps enormously to focus and calm the mind. In deep meditation visions occur spontaneously and God often appears to saints in this manner. By visualizing an expansive scene we build a bridge from individual to universal consciousness.

A very powerful way to start meditation is by visualizing an expanding light. After you have calmed and centered yourself, picture a blue light at the point between the eyebrows. When you can visualize the light clearly, let it expand, filling first all the cells of your brain, and then gradually infusing every atom of your body. See it continue to expand until it fills the room in which you are sitting, then your whole house, your neighborhood, your state, your country, and finally the whole earth. As if from outer space, watch the earth floating in a sea of blue light. Feel that this light is uniting everyone and everything, creating harmony and love. Now, continue to expand the light until it fills the whole solar system, then the whole of the universe. See the stars as little points of white light floating in an ocean of blue light. Feel that you, too, are floating in that sea of light and, in fact, *are* that light. Your body has become the universe and everything in it. The stars are your cells. Feel the great peace, security, and joy of this state. You need nothing because you *have* everything. Nothing can harm you because you are everything. Float in the joy of this universal consciousness for as long as you can, and then gradually let the light condense until it again becomes a spot at the point between the eyebrows. This and several other visualizations by Kriyananda are available on tape with beautiful background music. (See *Resources* section.)

One of the best things to visualize is simply the face, and especially the eyes, of Jesus Christ, Yogananda, or another saint. The eyes are the "windows of the soul," and by visualizing those of a master one becomes attuned to his consciousness. Try to see them very clearly, first by looking at a picture, and then by visualizing them until they come alive inside your mind. Commune with them, sending and receiving love and attunement.

Techniques to interiorize and concentrate the mind will normally take up the greater part of a meditation. Don't stop practicing these techniques too soon. Only when you are deeply concentrated and feeling a state of divine awareness is it good to drop techniques and simply immerse yourself in the experience. If any restlessness remains, they will be the means of going deeper. Do concentration techniques for at least a quarter to a third of your time, more if you are not also doing other meditation techniques. On the other hand, concentrating the mind should not consume all of your time, but should lead to the next stage, expansion. At least the final quarter of your meditation should be spent in silent inner communion with God and your higher self.

Expansion

SECTION THREE

Expansion

The final stage of meditation is the expansion of consciousness. In fact, until this expansion has taken place, we are not truly meditating. In his booklet, *Metaphysical Meditations*, Yogananda writes, "Meditation is not the same as concentration. Concentration consists in freeing the attention from objects of distraction and focusing it on one thing at a time. Meditation is that special form of concentration in which the attention has been liberated from restlessness and is focused on God. A man may *concentrate* on the thought of Divinity or of money; but he may not *meditate* on money or any other material thing. Meditation is focused only on thoughts of God and His holy prophets."

This distinction is vital. Concentration, a mental facility, can be merely an extension of the ego and therefore lead us further into delusion, whereas true meditation involves the superconscious and will always lead us toward truth. It is through opening ourselves to God that we draw the grace that changes us. The stage of expansion requires a merging of our individual consciousness with God or one of His qualities.

After achieving a state of deep concentration, we should spend as long as possible in an expansive state of consciousness. Expansion can be experienced through both devotion and inner communion. Each involves keeping the already concentrated mind focused on God.

Devotion

Devotion is love that has been purified and offered to God. Usually it involves the worship of one of His incarnations. Thus a Christian might worship Christ or possibly one of the saints. A Hindu would likely worship Shiva, Vishnu, Krishna, or some other form of the Godhead. Those who have found a guru might worship God as He manifests through that soul. Even though one religion or master may particularly appeal to you, it is good to remember that there is but one God who has manifested in every form. He is equally present in all religions and all souls. He is present in each of us as much as He is in the greatest saint. The difference is that they have realized it! As our devotion deepens, we should try to merge with the object of our devotion. Thus, the best way to worship Christ is to become Christ-like.

Outward worship often takes on elaborately ritualized ceremonies. These may help awaken zeal, but meditative devotion is much more inward. Try to attune yourself with *consciousness* rather than merely form. Try to commune with the master you are worshiping, drawing his or her consciousness into your own. Speak with him, share the innermost secrets of your heart. Give him your joys, your defeats, your possessions and attachments. Think of God in whatever form is dearest — mother, father, lover, friend. Finally, through your devotion, realize that you are one with the object of your worship.

There is a story told in India of a man who was worshiping his guru by offering rose petals before his picture. In the middle of his ceremony the man suddenly starting throwing the rose petals on his own head, saying, "I see now that I, untouched by ego consciousness, am that which I was worshiping. I bow to the Infinite Lord who has manifested in both my guru and in me."

Inner Communion

God manifests Himself through qualities as well as living forms. The Indian Scriptures teach that there are eight primary ways that God manifests: Light, Sound, Power, Wisdom, Calmness, Peace, Love, and Joy. A great expansion of consciousness takes place as we become absorbed in any of these qualities. After finishing the concentration techniques try to immerse yourself in whichever of these qualities most attracts you.

Saints of all ages and religions have experienced seeing a great light when in an ecstatic state. The Old and New

Testaments of the Bible have over a hundred references to light. The inner light of the spiritual eye will be seen in the forehead, at the point between the eyebrows, when the mind is calm and focused. This is the meaning of the passage in the Bible that says, "The light of the body is the eye: If therefore thine eye be single, thy whole body shall be full of light." (Matthew 6:22)

When the mind becomes very still you may see the spiritual eye itself, which appears as a white five-pointed star inside a blue field surrounded by a golden ring. If the mind is less calm, you may see a slightly distorted form of the spiritual eye such as a donut-shaped ring, or see just an intensification of light. Whatever you see, observe it calmly, increasing the intensity of your concentration until you become absorbed into the inner light.

It is very helpful to try to project your consciousness through the light into infinity beyond. In near death experiences, one of the things most commonly reported is traveling through a tunnel into a great light. This is also an experience common in deep meditation, when the energy is withdrawn from body consciousness and expanded into cosmic consciousness.

Sound and light are essentially the same — energy manifested through vibration. As in watching the inner light, you can listen to the inner sounds. Both techniques, while very rewarding, require considerable stillness of the mind. To hear the inner sounds more clearly, it is helpful to close the ears with the thumbs or use ear plugs. Whatever inner sound you hear, try to listen with great intensity, first becoming absorbed in the sound, and then feeling that it is dissolving all sense of ego and separation from God.

In attuning yourself with any aspect of God, be it light, love, joy, or any of the other qualities, start with what you are *already experiencing* and expand on that. The little light seen in the forehead can expand to become the light underlying the whole of creation. The smallest trace of love felt in the heart can be expanded until it embraces everyone you know, then all people, all creatures, and finally everything in creation, animate or inanimate. By absorbing the consciousness in any of these primary qualities one becomes attuned to God, who created them.

Intuitive Answers to Problems

Many people make the mistake of carrying their problems into their meditations. As long as the mind remains restless one will neither be able to meditate properly nor solve problems successfully. But once the mind has been focused and the consciousness expanded, the intuition becomes active and can be a great help in resolving life's dilemmas.

There is a technique to finding intuitive solutions to problems: First, try to simplify and clarify your question. Often an answer becomes obvious simply because the issue has been clarified. Next, ask the question at the spiritual eye as if you were broadcasting it to the universe. Ask with great intensity and with deep concentration, feeling that you are projecting the question through a tube at that point. Now, *expecting an answer,* concentrate either at the spiritual eye or at the heart center and listen very intently. Often you will simply know the answer to your question. If no solution comes, pose the most logical alternatives and *feel* the energy in the heart. Does one alternative produce a sense of nervousness and the other a feeling of peace? If so, try the solution that brings the peace. In order to be able to feel clearly you must be very objective. Holding on to an attachment or even a preference for one solution over another will inhibit the flow of intuition.

Always end your meditation with a prayer. You may want to pray for God's light to solve a difficulty or heal an illness if that is His will for you. Pray with the attitude that God *wants* to answer your prayer, that you are His own child, His dearest friend, and not some insignificant beggar. You may want to end your meditation by simply praying for the grace to be able to feel the peace and joy of meditation throughout your daily activities.

Transition to Activity

Carry the peace and joy you feel in meditation into your daily life. Stay quiet and centered following meditation, extending the calm into every aspect of life. When you realize that activity and meditation are really one you will be able to find a still center at the heart of even the most trying circumstances.

The first few minutes after meditation are especially important. Keep silence, if possible, and calmly go about your tasks while holding onto the inward feeling of meditation. Consciously feel that you are merely playing a role on God's stage. Realize that you own nothing and no one, but rather are the caretaker of those people and responsibilities He has placed in your hands. Often, after meditating, one finds colors to be brighter than normal, people to be more lovable, and events more in-joyable. Hold on to this portable paradise for as long as possible, extending it into your commute, your work place, your whole life. This practice will give you a still center during your daily duties and an amazing strength during times of trial.

In 1976 a forest fire destroyed virtually every home at Ananda. In the tense hours of the inferno and the confusing days that followed, the residents of the community were calm and even happy, never losing their center or their sense of humor. Our family lived in a geodesic dome that was esthetically open and inviting. Unfortunately, its seams were also open and inviting. In short, it leaked like a sieve. After fighting the fire for several hours and watching our home burn to the ground, I finally returned to where my wife, Devi, and our ten-day-old son were waiting. My words of greeting were, "Well, we don't have to worry about leaks anymore." Within minutes we were talking calmly about the "tragedy" and planning optimistically for the future.

For our family and other residents of Ananda, the daily practice of meditation had produced a state of non-attachment and inner joy which easily withstood what, for others in our area, was a major life test. In the days and months following the fire we saw the fulfillment of God's promise in the *Bhagavad Gita:* "Even a little practice of this inward religion will free one from dire fears and colossal sufferings."

The Basic Routine for Meditation

Relaxation

Before you sit to meditate you may want to stretch and relax by doing a few rounds of the deep yogic breath and/or the corpse pose.

As you sit, check your posture. Be sure the spine is erect, the chest up and the shoulders slightly back. Relax the abdomen and check to see that you are breathing from the diaphragm.

Offer a prayer to God, to those souls who particularly inspire you, and to your own higher self. Ask for the grace to be able to go into deep meditation and inner communion with God.

Inhale with a double breath, tense the whole body until it vibrates, throw the breath out with a double exhalation, and relax completely. Repeat three to six times.

Consciously relax all the parts of the body, starting at the feet and working your way up, part by part, to the head. End by relaxing the brain.

Practice six to nine rounds of *regular breathing* to relax and focus the mind. Inhale counting to twelve, hold for a count of twelve, exhale to the same twelve count. The rhythm can be shorter or longer according to your capacity, but be sure to keep the inhalation, holding and exhalation equal. From this point on try not to move any part of the body until you have finished the meditation.

Concentrate at the point between the eyebrows. Dismiss all thoughts from the mind and be completely centered in the here and now. Don't think about the past or worry about the future.

Excluding the stretching before you sit to meditate, the process of relaxation should take only five to ten minutes.

Interiorization

Practice one or more of the techniques of concentration. You could start with *chanting*. First chant vigorously in order to awaken greater energy. Gradually become more and more inward until you go beyond the words into the silent yearning of heart and soul.

You may also want to do a *visualization exercise*. This can be done either silently within or by listening to a recorded visualization.

Now practice the technique of *watching the breath* for approximately one fourth of your total meditation time. Try to bring your mind to a state of total concentration. If you find that your mind has wandered, gently bring it back to the technique. Try to deepen your concentration until you become completely absorbed and the breath becomes still. End the technique by inhaling deeply and exhaling three times.

Expansion

Hold onto the state of deep concentration and calmness for as long as possible, trying always to go deeper into the inner silence. Gradually shift from the active "doing" state of practicing techniques to the receptive "being" state.

Inwardly attune yourself to the presence of God, one of His saints, or one of His eight qualities. If you feel particularly drawn to a personal incarnation of God or a guru, try to feel his inward touch. Or you may prefer in a particular meditation to attune yourself to one of God's impersonal manifestations: light, sound, love, joy, etc. Whether communing with God in a personal or impersonal form, try to dissolve all sense of individuality and separation. Become one with the object of your meditation! Hold this state for as long as you can.

While still in the state of deep calmness you may want to *ask for help or guidance* concerning problems you are experiencing in your life. Broadcast your question from the spiritual eye and listen there or in the heart center for the answer. Expect an answer!

End your meditation with a prayer for yourself, for those close to you, and for the whole world. Pray, too, for the grace to feel His presence throughout all your activities.

Try always to *keep your meditations fresh, energetic, and intuitive.* Too little use of techniques will result in shallow meditations, but too much routine will make your meditations dry. Try to find the balance that brings you the most joy. Joy is the hallmark of proper meditation.

Application

SECTION FOUR

Application

While meditation is, by its nature, a time spent apart from the concerns of daily living, there are numerous ways that the tools learned in meditation can be applied to daily life. Among the most important areas are relationships, work, and health and healing.

Relationships

Little else in life brings us as much joy or as much pain as our relationships with others. We are constantly seeking fulfillment through our friends, co-workers, and spouse. Yet most of the "choices" we make in our relationships are conditioned by individual past tendencies operating on a subconscious level, and by the magnetism of the cultural environment we live in. Most of the time we react rather than act. Meditation centers us, strengthens our powers of discrimination, and reduces our vulnerability to the hidden persuaders of society. Through meditation we are able to become a cause rather than an effect. This is especially helpful for improving relationships.

Ideally, we should become more aware of both our own selves and others as souls rather than bodies and personalities. This perspective can be gained through deep meditation, and as we become centered in this way, profound changes can happen in the way we relate to others. Instead of demanding, even subconsciously, that others fulfill our "needs," we find fulfillment from within. Cooperation replaces competition; the joy of mutual giving replaces the friction of reciprocating demands. A great sense of contentment comes as we realize that relationships are given to us primarily to help *us* learn and grow, especially to grow in our ability to accept and to love. The marriage vows we take at Ananda end with:

> *"May our love grow ever deeper, purer, more expansive, until, in our perfected love, we find the perfect love of God."*

Relationships begun in this manner hold the promise of deep fulfillment. There is a technique for attracting the right life partner that can be done in meditation. After you have achieved a state of deep calmness, concentrate at the spiritual eye and send out a soul call to God to send you an ideal mate. Don't concentrate at all on physical appearance, but only on the soul qualities. Now send out strong energy in the form of magnetism to attract a mate with qualities ideally suited to you and your journey to God. As your concentration and energy level become ever more intense, the power of the magnetism will increase. Eventually, if the magnetism is strong enough, this "soul call" will find a responsive chord in someone else and you will be drawn together.

This technique can be used to draw not only a mate. Once, during the depression era, Paramhansa Yogananda talked about using this power to find work. He told his audience, many of them out of work, that if he didn't have a job, he would concentrate at the spiritual eye and churn the ether until the universe gave him one.

Work

Work should be seen as a joyous opportunity for self-expression and growth, a kind of meditation in action. There is a branch of yoga, called *karma yoga,* which has as its ideal "action without any desire for the fruits of the action." How different this is from the typical modern day job so often fraught with boredom, clock watching, office politics, and antagonism between workers and management. Ask yourself this question: If you did not have to work for economic reasons, would you continue in your present job? Would you continue to work at all? If the answer is no there is something wrong with your job or, more likely, your attitude toward it.

Our work should be seen in terms of what we can give to it rather than what we get from it; in terms of personal growth rather than personal reward. A few years ago at Ananda we were rebuilding houses that had been burnt in a devastating forest fire. Everyone was pitching in, and consequently we had people on the carpentry crews who could be described charitably as less than totally qualified. One day as we broke from work for lunch, everyone was discouraged because we could see that we were actually farther behind than when we had started the day. The head carpenter on the project gave us all both encouragement and a chuckle by saying, "Well, let's remember that we're not building houses, we're building character."

In addition to having proper attitudes, the techniques we learned for meditation can be carried over into the workplace. In fact, the three stages of meditation (relaxation, concentration, and expansion) should also be applied to the workplace. The same techniques that we use to relax before meditating can be applied in a modified form while at work. Good posture, deep breathing, and gentle stretching will help you stay physically relaxed. Pausing for a moment to close your eyes and watch the breath will immediately get you centered and concentrated again. When circumstances permit, a short meditation break at lunch time can be enormously helpful. Be expansive and creative in your work, making it primarily a way to learn and grow rather than a way to earn a living.

Health and Healing

Paramhansa Yogananda said that the root cause of illness was the conflict between the soul and the ego — the soul trying to draw us toward an awareness of our unity with God and the ego trying to convince us that we are separate individuals. The subconscious tension created by this opposition produces blockages in the flow of life-force and ultimately disease, since good health depends upon a strong unobstructed flow of life-force to all areas of the body. Illness, moods, apathy — in fact all negative states — are symptoms of a conflict or blockage in the flow of our life-force. One of the great benefits of meditation is that through a deep integration of our consciousness, we are gradually freed from these conflicts and experience our natural state, which is one of vibrant health and energy.

Usually life-force flows where it is needed without conscious control or even awareness on our part. But it is possible, through the use of will and yogic techniques, to override the automatic, unconscious process and direct life-force wherever we want: to energize the whole system, heal an injured or diseased area, or even heal others. Will is the master switch that draws this *prana* into the body from its universal source and directs it to flow to wherever it is needed. The connection between will and life-force is especially important in healing. The next time you are unwell, try using this technique for healing:

Concentrate at the medulla oblongata (the part of the brain at the base of the skull), touching the area once in order to make it easier for you to focus on it. Visualize light entering both at that point and at the spiritual eye and pouring down the spine. Now begin to gently tense and relax the whole body in order to flood it with life-force. Using your will, direct a flow of life-force from the medulla down the arms and into the hands. Continue gently tensing and relaxing the body, and feeling the energy flow from the medulla and spiritual eye through the spine and into the hands.

Now stop tensing and relaxing, and rub the bared skin of the left arm with the right hand. Do the same on the other side. Relax a moment while continuing to visualize the flow of *prana* into the hands. Now rub the hands gently but briskly together. The hands are very magnetic and have a polarity, the left hand being a south pole and the right hand a north pole. Rubbing them together crosses the poles and, as in a generator, produces a flow of energy. Raise your arms, hands upward, and feel the tingling sensation of the life-force flowing into them.

Place your hands on or near the area you want to heal and, using them as power sources, send healing life-force into the afflicted cells in a continuous stream. Continue until you feel you have filled the area with light. Do this technique several times per day until the healing is finished. I know of many seemingly miraculous stories attesting to the effectiveness of this procedure.

A member of Ananda was once taking a day hike on a glacier in Canada. After several hours of walking, he slipped in a crevasse and sprained his ankle very severely. It was so badly swollen that it was painful to put any weight on it and impossible to try to walk. But the alternative was freezing to death after night fell. He sat on his pack, placed his hands on his ankle and, for the next half hour, with deep concentration, sent energy to the injured limb using the technique described above. After that time he was able to walk with very little pain. A day or two later his ankle was completely healed.

Several years ago another member of Ananda, a doctor, was in a very bad car accident in an isolated area of Mexico. Even though she had a crushed pelvis and nearly every bone in her legs was broken, it was almost 24 hours before she was able to reach a hospital. The doctor who operated on her said there was no chance that she would ever be able to walk again. During her recuperation, she used these life-force techniques every day, sometimes for several hours at a time, to send energy to her injured legs. The whole hospital was absolutely amazed at her rate of recovery. She went home after three months and today she walks with only a very slight limp.

This same energy can be used to heal others as well as yourself. After you have energized the hands and can feel the flow of *prana* in them, place them on the part of the person to which you are wanting to send energy. Concentrate on the *flow* of energy, feeling it as warmth, or visualizing it as light. Pray that God's healing power pass through you and into the person needing the energy.

Distance is no barrier to this energy, so this technique can also be used to heal people at a distance. In such cases, strongly visualize the person to whom you are sending the energy. After magnetizing your hands move them up and down in space, sending waves of energy and willing the current to pass into the recipient's diseased part. Continue this procedure for fifteen minutes or until you feel you have accomplished your purpose. In a public situation where it would be awkward to use the hands, you can simply feel energy flowing from your spiritual eye into the spiritual eye of the other person.

The connection between will and energy is a universal one and has applications in many areas of life other than healing. It is especially applicable to the rejuvenation and energization of the body and mind. Paramhansa Yogananda devised a wonderful system called the Energization Exercises, which takes advantage of the power of will to draw life-force into the body.

The Energization Exercises

The Energization Exercises is a systematic method to increase the flow of life-force and send it to every area of the body in order to strengthen and energize it. These exercises also clear and strengthen the mind. While the whole system of 39 exercises should be learned from a qualified instructor, the principles and two of the main exercises are given here.

1) Concentrate primarily on the *flow* of energy. Focus your attention at the medulla oblongata at the base of the skull and feel that you are drawing energy from the universe into your body through that point. (Just as food enters our body through our mouth, *prana* enters through an energy center, or *chakra,* whose physical counterpart is the medulla.) Now, through the use of your will, and by alternately tensing and relaxing the appropriate body part, direct energy to flow into that part and energize the cells. After tensing an area, relax and feel the result. This not only recharges the body with energy but, even more importantly, trains us to bring the flow of *prana* under our conscious control. Concentrate very deeply during the practice of these exercises, even closing your eyes to help deepen and interiorize your awareness.

2) The tensing and relaxing of the muscles should be done in phases so as not to "strip" them. Tense: low — slight tension, medium — significant tension but not as strong as, high — strong enough to cause the body part to vibrate. Hold high tension for only three to four seconds. Tense in a continuous wave: low, medium, high, and relax back in a wave: high, medium, low, completely relaxed. Concentrate on the center of the muscle or muscle group

to which you are sending the energy and always practice slowly, smoothly, and with deep concentration.

3) There is a spiritual law: "The greater the will, the greater the flow of energy." Feel that, through the agency of your will, you are consciously drawing and directing a limitless stream of energy. While it is better to think of will as "willingness" in order to avoid making it seem grim, you should use your will very intensely, especially while tensing any area. Try also to be intensely aware as you relax and feel the result.

4) If a body part is ill or injured, use low tension only. Using low tension, send energy to that part counting slowly to ten. Repeat this several times. For internal organs or body parts which you can't feel you can send the energy only mentally. It may be helpful to visualize a current of light flowing to the affected part.

5) Begin with a prayer: "Beloved Indweller, Great Spirit, manifest Thy spirit in this body as strength and energy, in this mind as concentration and determination, and in this soul as ever-increasing, ever-new joy."

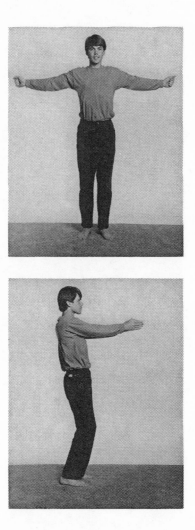

Double Breathing
(with palms touching)

With your arms out straight to your sides at shoulder level, exhale with the double breath[*] and bring your arms to the front until your palms touch. With a double inhalation, bring your arms back out — tensing the entire body upwards in a wave. Relax down in reverse order with the double exhalation. **Do this five times.**

*Double breathing is done by inhaling through the nose with a short inhalation followed immediately by a longer one in a huh/huuuuhh rhythm. Exhale through both the nose and mouth in the same huh/huuuuhh way.

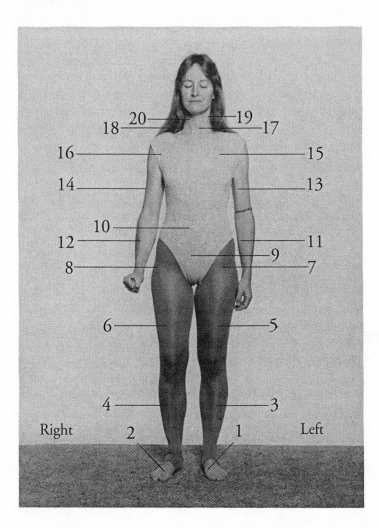

Twenty-Part Body Recharging

a) Inhale with a double inhalation. As you do so, tense your whole body hard enough so the body vibrates. Hold the tension for three to five seconds, then exhale with a double exhalation and relax.

b) Individually tense and then relax the twenty body parts in order:

1) left foot	8) right buttock	15) left chest
2) right foot	9) abdomen (below navel)	16) right chest
3) left calf	10) stomach (above navel)	17) left of neck
4) right calf	11) left forearm	18) right of neck
5) left thigh	12) right forearm	19) back of neck
6) right thigh	13) left upper arm	20) front of neck
7) left buttock	14) right upper arm	

c) Quickly tense (only to medium tension) in order the same twenty body parts, holding the tension in each part as you go up the body. Inhale slowly as you do so. Now inhale completely and tense the whole body hard enough to vibrate.

d) Relax the neck, dropping the chin to the chest. Then exhale slowly while relaxing the remaining body parts in reverse order.

The Spinal Centers

As we discussed, *prana* flows into the body through the medulla oblongata. *Prana* is not physical energy, but a form of subtle (astral) energy. Once this energy enters, it travels down the *astral spine* and is dispersed into the body from six centers or *chakras* located along the astral spine. This subtle spine can be visualized as a tube of light running through the center of the body from the brain to the base of the spine.

There is a vast and rather complex yogic science dealing with the *chakras*. Each *chakra* is associated with a human drive; an element; a planet; two astrological signs (one as the energy ascends and one as it descends); a sound; a spiritual quality; and so forth. As energy passes through (or rests in) any *chakra* the mind is influenced by the qualities of that center. In the deepest states of meditation all *prana* is withdrawn from both the physical and astral bodies and uplifted into the spiritual eye, enabling enlightenment to take place.

The body is sustained primarily by *prana* and only secondarily by food, water, and air. It is even possible to live only by *prana* and dispense with food altogether. Paramhansa Yogananda, in his spiritual classic, *Autobiography of a Yogi,* gives examples of several people who learned to exist on subtle energy alone and no longer needed to eat at all. He writes at length of his visit to the great Catholic visionary, Therese Neumann, who lived her entire adult life eating nothing but a single communion wafer each day. This sustenance through *prana* is the mystical meaning of Christ's statement in Luke 4:4 when, after fasting for forty days, he answers the temptation of the devil to turn stones into bread by saying, "It is written, that man shall not live by bread alone, but by every word that proceedeth from the mouth of God." Christ was able to consciously draw that energy, or word of God, and no longer needed to be kept alive by food.

In the unenlightened man *prana* is involuntarily directed downward from the medulla into the astral spine. An enlightened master, however, is able to direct the life-force from the medulla to the spiritual eye. From that point, if he so chooses, he can command it to descend into the body to carry out the necessary physical functions. Because the energy is under the control of the superconscious, it doesn't create identification with the ego, or *karma*. When a master wants to withdraw his consciousness from this world, he simply wills the *prana* to be redirected to the spiritual eye.

Our language contains a hidden wisdom concerning the directional flow of our energy. The upward flow of *prana* is associated with uplifted and expansive states of consciousness, while the downward flow produces negative and contractive states. We are "uplifted," or "high," or "on cloud nine" when our energy is flowing in an upward direction. The word *inspiration* means both upliftment of consciousness and inhalation. On the other hand we can feel "low," "down," or "in the dumps" when our *prana* is flowing more strongly than usual in a downward, negative direction.

Our body language also unconsciously reflects this. When we are feeling inspired we tend to emphasize the upward flow by sitting up straight and by inhaling deeply. But when depressed, we slump and emphasize the downward flow with a sigh. Saints in ecstasy are pictured with their eyes uplifted, the normal position of the eyes in a state of superconsciousness. The nimbus, or halo, seen in paintings of saints is symbolic of their energy having been lifted up to the top of the head and expanded.

But lest we get caught in the mere complexity of it all, it would be well to remember that in meditation we are dealing with a simple process. Concentrate your mind one-pointedly on God and everything else will take care of itself. As Yogananda's guru, Swami Sri Yukteswar, once said to him, "God is simple. All else is complex."

The following is a summation of the spinal centers and their qualities. For those who would like to delve more deeply into this fascinating science, Kriyananda devotes two lessons to them in his course, *Lessons in Yoga: Fourteen Steps to Higher Awareness.*

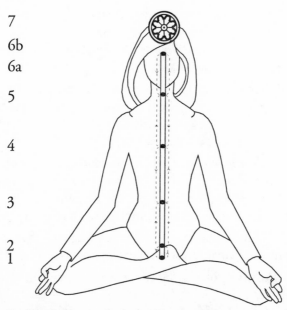

1) *Muladhara chakra:* Coccyx center, at the base of the spine. *Element:* Earth. *Human drive:* Security. *Spiritual quality:* Power to follow rules of *yama* (see next section). *Manifestation of the AUM sound:* Bumblebee. *Planet:* Saturn. *Astrological signs:* Aquarius and Capricorn.

2) *Swadistan chakra:* Sacral center, in the spine opposite the reproductive organs. *Element:* Water. *Human drive:* Sexuality. *Spiritual quality:* Power to follow rules of *niyama. AUM sound:* Flute. *Planet:* Jupiter. *Astrological signs:* Pisces and Sagittarius.

3) *Manipur chakra:* Lumbar center, opposite the navel. *Element:* Fire. *Human drive:* Power. *Spiritual quality:* Fiery self-control. *AUM sound:* Harp. *Planet:* Mars. *Astrological signs:* Scorpio and Aries.

4) *Anahat chakra:* Dorsal center, opposite the heart. *Element:* Air. *Human drive:* Love. *Spiritual quality:* Divine love. *AUM sound:* Bells. *Planet:* Venus. *Astrological signs:* Libra and Taurus.

5) *Vishudha chakra:* Cervical center, opposite the throat. *Element:* Ether. *Human drive:* Calmness. *Spiritual quality:* Calmness. *AUM sound:* Wind. *Planet:* Mercury. *Astrological signs:* Gemini and Virgo.

6a) **Negative pole:** Medulla oblongata. *Spiritual quality:* Ego. *Planet:* Moon. Astrological sign: Cancer.

6b) **Positive pole:** *Ajna chakra:* Christ center, at the point between the eyebrows. *Element:* Super-ether. *Human drive:* Joy. Spiritual qualities: Joy, divine will, soul consciousness. *AUM sound:* AUM. *Planet:* Sun. *Astrological sign:* Leo.

7) *Sahasrara:* Thousand-petaled lotus, at the top of the head. Center of divine union. This center opens up only after the energy has been completely raised to the Christ center.

In order to become more aware of the astral spine you might do the following: Place your left hand at the base of the spine and your right hand at the medulla oblongata (in the "hollow" at the base of the skull). Visualize a tube of light, like a fluorescent tube, connecting these two points. It may help you to feel this tube more clearly if you sway your body gently from side to side while resisting the movement slightly. Now take your left hand and place it at the point between the eyebrows, visualizing the tube bending at the medulla and flowing through the brain to the frontal lobe. This "tube" is the astral spine.

One of the most effective techniques for working with the spinal centers is the chanting of AUM at the *chakras*. Start at the coccyx center, at the base of the spine, and slowly work your way up, mentally chanting AUM at each *chakra*. As you do so, try to actually *feel* energy at that point. It will help if you feel that the sound of AUM and even your breath is emanating from that center. When you reach the point between the eyebrows, concentrate there for a time and then slowly work your way down, again mentally chanting AUM at each *chakra*. Kriyananda has ascribed a particular note of the scale to each *chakra:* coccyx—G, sacral—A, lumbar—B flat, dorsal—D, cervical—E flat, medulla—F, Christ center—G.

Another very valuable technique is to simply listen, after the mind has been calmed and interiorized, to the inner sounds. As listed above, each *chakra* has a particular sound associated with it. By listening very intently to these inner sounds, we are able to attune ourselves to the very creative force of the universe, known in Christian literature as the Holy Ghost, or "The Comforter."

Patanjali's Eightfold Path

The meditation techniques we have been learning are part of the larger science of *raja* (royal) *yoga*. It is a science which includes all other branches of yoga within it, just as a king includes all provinces within his kingdom. *Raja yoga's* first written expression was by an ancient master, Patanjali.

Patanjali is the most revered of all the ancient exponents of yoga. Writing a few centuries before Christ, he explained yoga so succinctly that every teacher, be he scholar or saint, regards his *Yoga Sutras* as the "scripture" of yoga. His *Yoga Sutras* consist of a series of 196 very pithy statements or aphorisms, often only a single sentence long. These cover not only the path of yoga, but also the nature of the mind and, indeed, the whole of the human condition. Far more than mere philosophical speculation, the *Sutras* serve as a road map for those who would explore the realm of Self-realization. Patanjali was an enlightened master, writing from a state of realization and practical knowledge. Other great saints who have followed the path of yoga to its end have experienced the same metaphysical mysteries that Patanjali wrote about.

Patanjali's definition of yoga (or union) is both simple and profound. He says yoga is "the cessation of the fluctuations of mind-stuff." The implications of this are vast. In order to achieve a state of union we need no book learning, nor need we participate in any prescribed rituals, nor join any church, nor achieve any exalted position. As soon as we can control the fluctuations of our mind (Yogananda interpreted this to mean especially our attachments), we automatically awaken to our true state — that of unity with the Infinite. We are, in our intrinsic nature, an extension of God, rather than sinners forever damned to be separate from Him.

In one section of the *Yoga Sutras,* called *ashtanga* (eight-limbed) *yoga,* Patanjali outlines the steps that lead to cosmic consciousness. A brief review of these eight steps will serve as a guide to the science of *raja yoga.* As you shall see, this path is the one presented in this book and consists of interiorizing one's energy, concentrating one's mind, and expanding one's consciousness until it becomes infinite. But the ability to do this, as in all things on the path to Self-realization, comes through God's grace, and therefore Paramhansa Yogananda taught that everything, even breathing techniques, should be done with deep devotion.

Patanjali's first two steps or branches tell us the rules and attitudes we should use to guide our lives. It does little good to gather the milk of peace in meditation if the bucket of our life is so full of holes that the precious milk drains out immediately. Westerners might tend to think of the first two steps, the *yamas* and *niyamas,* as being similar to the Ten Commandments of the Bible. But rather than commandments, they are better seen as the basic attitudes necessary in order to be in harmony with the universal order. To practice the *yamas* and *niyamas* properly one must understand that they require correcting both outward behavior and inner attitudes.

The next three steps cover the process of internalizing *prana,* first by holding the body perfectly still (*asana*), then by controlling the flow of life-force (*pranayama*), and finally by withdrawing energy from the senses (*pratyahara*).

Patanjali's final three limbs cover the focusing and expansion of consciousness. The withdrawal of the life-force allows us to achieve a state of complete concentration (*dharana*). Through holding a state of total concentration, we shift our sense of self-identity, breaking the chains of ego identification, and become one with the object of our concentration (*dhyana*). Finally, realizing we are no longer bound by the ego, our consciousness expands to merge with all of creation (*samadhi*). The state of *samadhi* is beyond what the common man even dreams of, and yet it is the ultimate destiny of every one of us.

Yama, Niyama — Right Behavior

Yama. These are, literally, the *controls* or don'ts of life. They include areas where we must learn to control tendencies which, if allowed expression, would end up causing us disharmony and pain. The *yamas* are a) nonviolence; b) non-lying; c) non-stealing; d) non-sensuality; and e) non-greed.

a) **Non-Violence** (*Ahimsa*). As in all the *yamas* and *niyamas*, the goal is to achieve not only outer control but, more importantly, a completely natural inner state of compliance. Thus, if we are to practice non-violence properly, we must not only refrain outwardly from harming or demeaning any living thing, but we must also accomplish the more difficult task of overcoming any tendency to *wish* harm. When these inner, often subconscious, tendencies that have kept us captive in our isolated egos are finally quelled, we achieve a wondrous harmony with all life, and perfect inner freedom. In fact, Patanjali says that when one perfects any of the *yamas* or *niyamas*, a special power or *siddhi* comes. When one perfects the quality of non-violence, all the world becomes peaceful around him.

b) **Non-Lying** (*Satya*). First, learn to control any tendency to *say* anything that is not truthful. Then, also practice complete inward honesty. Without complete self-honesty we can't hope to perceive ultimate Truth. The power that comes with the perfection of *satya* is that whatever one says will come true.

c) **Non-Stealing** (*Astaya*). Curb the tendency to take anything that does not belong to you. This includes not only material objects, but also more subtle things such as praise or position. On the level of human relationships, it means not to try to take energy, or even love, from someone unless it has been freely offered. The power that comes with perfection of this quality is that any wealth that is needed comes automatically.

d) Non-Sensuality (*Brahmacharya*). Learn the art of self-control. Tremendous energy is expended through seeking or thinking about sensual pleasures. While this *yama* refers specifically to sexual self-control, it also includes other sense pleasures. Rather than dealing with the question of the rightness or sinfulness of sexuality, yoga deals with the question of how we want to direct our energy. The *siddhi* that comes when we learn not to waste our energy through the senses is tremendous mental and spiritual vitality.

e) Non-Greed (*Aparigraha*). Learn not to be attached to or desirous of even that which you could rightly claim to be yours. Discriminate between "needs" and "wants." Greed stems from some level of insecurity, and as we mature spiritually we develop a deep faith in the power of the universe to sustain us. In deep meditation we see that we are now, always have been, and always shall be sustained only through the outpouring of God's energy. The power that comes with the perfection of non-greed is that when you no longer are attached to, or identified with, yourself as you now are, you can see your past, present, and future lives clearly.

Niyama. The *niyamas* are the non-controls or the dos of the path. These are the areas of our life we need to develop, and into which we should allow our energy to flow. The *niyamas* are a) cleanliness; b) contentment; c) austerity; d) self-study; and e) devotion to God.

a) **Cleanliness** (*Saucha*). Purity of body, mind, and environment is very important for harmonizing our energies. An Indian saint, Swami Chidananda, once visited Ananda, and upon seeing a rusty watering can lying in the garden remarked, "You should pick that up and paint it. Lower entities are attracted to clutter." The power that comes with perfection of cleanliness is a divine indifference to things related to the body.

b) **Contentment** (*Santosha*). It is a supreme virtue to be able to accept things as they are and to be content. Yet this virtue does not imply that one can become apathetic or lazy. The power that comes with perfection is supreme happiness.

c) **Austerity** (*Tapasya*). We must learn to be master over our likes and dislikes and have the strength of determination to do what we decide. Traditionally this *niyama* means to perfect our ability to perform austerities — the Indian scriptures are full of stories about saints who gained magical powers through the performance of austerity. But while these stories seem at first reading to be talking about power over the world around us, the deeper understanding is that they refer to power over our own ignorance. Patanjali says various psychic powers come with the perfection of this virtue.

d) Self-Study (*Swadhyaya*). Introspection allows us to see how God has chosen to manifest Himself in this form that we call ourself. Introspection need not imply any negative judgment about ourselves or our qualities, but rather the ability to be completely clear-minded and objective. Without introspection it is next to impossible to progress on the spiritual path. The power that comes with perfection is the vision of that aspect of God that one worships.

e) Devotion (*Iswara Pranidhana*). Devotion is the turning of the natural love of the heart toward God rather than toward the objects of the world. It is the one quality that is absolutely essential if we are to progress on the spiritual path. If our devotion is strong enough we will somehow manage, as many Christian saints have demonstrated, to achieve our goal even without techniques. Perfect devotion brings the supreme state — *samadhi,* or divine bliss.

The *yamas* and *niyamas*, Patanjali says, must not be "conditioned by class, place, time, or occasion." He implies that we must not find excuses to avoid doing what is right. If we sincerely try to practice these qualities, inevitably there will arise occasions that make us doubt that it is possible. Yet, if we persevere, it is the universe, not we, that will have to readjust. This is a profound and subtle teaching which forms the basis of the law of miracles. It is our consciousness, working through subtle laws of magnetism, that *creates* our circumstances just as it is God's consciousness that creates the universe as a whole. Consciousness, not form, has the central role. God's consciousness, acting through a pure channel (one firmly established in the *yamas* and *niyamas*), has the power to work any miracle imaginable.

The study and practice of these ten precepts is worthy of a lifetime of effort and, if attempted, will certainly change your life. Imagine what a paradise this earth would be if people everywhere dedicated themselves to these principles.

Asana, Pranayama, Pratyahara — Interiorization

Asana (posture) is the next limb. Patanjali says simply, "The posture should be steady and comfortable. From this comes freedom from the assaults of the pairs of opposites."

In order to accomplish perfect physical stillness it helps greatly if the body is strong, flexible, and healthy. The whole science of *hatha yoga* (yoga postures) evolved from the simple need to keep the body completely still during the long periods of meditation needed to attain cosmic consciousness. When practiced correctly, *hatha yoga* is a marvelous science which produces amazing fitness not only for the muscles and joints, but also for the internal organs. But *hatha yoga* goes far beyond mere physical benefits because, as a true yoga, it works with the life-force and therefore affects the body, the mind, and the spirit. In Kriyananda's system of *Yoga Postures for Higher Awareness,* these more subtle benefits are emphasized. Each posture is given an affirmation designed to increase the natural flow of *prana* produced by that particular pose.

Hatha yoga has become, unfortunately, something of a religion in itself in recent years. Wonderful though it is, it should always be seen in perspective. Its purpose, and the purpose of every activity undertaken by the true seeker, is to help us find God. One time a *hatha yoga* adept came to give a demonstration of the postures to the great woman saint, Anandamayee Ma. As he was going expertly through a series of extremely difficult postures, Ma sat quietly staring off into space, hardly even bothering to recognize his presence. "Why," she was saying through her silence, "should I pay any attention to this egotist who has perverted even this holy science into just another way of puffing up his pride?" In the practice of the *asana*s, as in all things, let us reflect the words of Yogananda's beautiful poem:

> *In waking, eating, working, dreaming, sleeping,*
> *Serving, meditating, chanting, divinely loving,*
> *My soul will constantly hum, unheard by any:*
> *God! God! God!*

Pranayama (energy control) is the next limb. As we discussed earlier, *pranayama* is control of the energy in the body, both physical and subtle. In earlier sections we learned techniques to become aware of, and to be able to direct, the flow of life-force. Patanjali says that in order to achieve a state of deep meditation, the life-force must become internalized.

Pratyahara (sense control), Patanjali says, is the "withdrawing of the mind and senses from the objects of the senses. Then follows the greatest mastery over the senses."

Paramhansa Yogananda called this stage "shutting off the sense telephones." In meditation it is helpful to do whatever you can to shut off the outward sensory stimuli. Many people who practice meditation use ear plugs or headphones to reduce sound, since hearing is the most likely of all the senses to disturb meditation. Yet one can only go so far to shut off *outward* causes of distraction. I remember once, under very silent conditions, being disturbed by the sound my eyelashes made when I blinked! True *pratyahara* is practiced in the mind, not the body. It is the internalization of the life-force which shuts off the sense telephones. But for deep interiorization we must also withdraw the *mind* from its tendency toward restlessness. This is done through concentration, Patanjali's sixth step.

Dharana, Dhyana, Samadhi — Expansion Through Meditation

Dharana (Concentration). This is the ability to bring the mind into focus and to hold the concentration on a single point. As we truly achieve this stage, all body consciousness and thoughts will cease and we will be completely focused on the object of our meditation. If, for instance, we are seeing a light at the spiritual eye, we will have no restlessness of the mind to disturb us. The goal of watching the breath is to achieve the state of *dharana*.

Dhyana (Absorption). Here we are speaking about the ability to merge with the object on which we are concentrating. In the state of *dhyana* we would merge into the light so completely that we would perceive ourself *as* that light. All would be light and we would no longer identify ourself as the perceiver, and the light as the object being perceived. The techniques given in the section on *Expansion* help one to achieve the state of *dhyana*.

Samadhi (Bliss). This refers to an expansion of consciousness so complete that there is Self-realization, a state of union with everything in creation and, finally, with God beyond creation. Having merged with the light we would come eventually to the realization that the whole of creation is made up of one light, and that our real nature is one of mystical union with everything and everyone.

Samadhi is a true state of union rather than an imaginary condition or even just an expanded sense of compassion for others. Yogananda, who had achieved the highest states of *samadhi*, knew the thoughts of all his students — not because he "read" their minds, but because he was *in* them as much as he was in his own body. One time he remarked to a student, "You have a sour taste in your mouth." When the student expressed astonishment, he explained, "I am as much in your mouth as I am in mine."

Kriyananda recounts the following incident in his wonderful book, *The Path — A Spiritual Autobiography*. It was during the time that Yogananda was in the desert writing his interpretations of the great scripture of India, the *Bhagavad Gita*.

> In the evenings, Master exercised by walking slowly around his retreat compound. Generally he asked me to accompany him. He was so much withdrawn from body-consciousness on those occasions that he sometimes had to lean on my arm for support. He would pause and sway back and forth, as if about to fall.
>
> "I am in so many bodies," Master remarked once, returning slowly to body-consciousness, "it is difficult for me to remember which body I am supposed to keep moving."

The attainment of this highest state of consciousness is the true goal of all life. It is from that state that we descended into form, and within each of us is the irrepressible yearning to return. All outward fulfillments are but pale reflections of the bliss of *samadhi.*

There are two major stages of *samadhi: sabikalpa samadhi,* in which the devotee must stay in a meditative state, and *nirbikalpa samadhi,* in which a great master can both function in the world and yet always stay in union with the Infinite. Yogananda's poem *Samadhi* is one of the clearest descriptions of this incredibly profound state that has ever been given in literature. He suggested that his disciples memorize it and recite it every day. His poem begins with these lines:

> *Vanished the veils of light and shade,*
> *Lifted every vapor of sorrow,*
> *Sailed away all dawns of fleeting joy,*
> *Gone the dim sensory mirage.*
>
> *Love, hate, health, disease, life, death,*
> *Perished these false shadows on the screen of duality.*
> *Waves of laughter, scyllas of sarcasm, melancholic*
>   *whirlpools,*
> *Melting in the vast sea of bliss.*
> *The storm of maya stilled,*
> *By magic wand of intuition deep.*
>
> *The universe, forgotten dream, subconsciously lurks,*
> *Ready to invade my newly wakened memory divine.*

I live without the cosmic shadow,
But it is not, bereft of me;
As the sea exists without the waves,
But they breathe not without the sea.

Dreams, wakings, states of deep turiya *sleep,*
Present, past, future, no more for me,
But ever-present, all-flowing I, I, everywhere.

It is this state of total union that is sought, consciously or unconsciously, by everyone. It is the ultimate goal of all life. And yet each of us has the free will to seek the "ever new, ever expanding joy" of *samadhi* or to turn, once again, toward the familiarity of old habits and attachments. The art and science of meditation beckons all those who choose to go toward the light.

While this book has been able to introduce you to some of the most powerful techniques in yoga, nothing can be a substitute for actual practice. Two aids are especially important. First in importance is attuning your will with God. In order to be able to do this it is extremely helpful to have a teacher or *guru.*

Second in importance, according to the scriptures of India, is the company of other truth seekers. Seek out companions who will be an aid to your search for the Infinite. Ananda has centers and meditation groups around the world where you can find guidance and encouragement. We also have a meditation retreat, *The Expanding Light*, where we offer classes in meditation and many other subjects. If you would like more information, please write us at Ananda, 14618 Tyler Foote Road, Nevada City, California, 95959.

May you, friend, be blessed, through your practice of meditation, with enlightenment — the true goal of all life. I pray that God shower you with His grace and that His Light illumine your pathway home.

About the Author

John (Jyotish) Novak is a close friend and student of Kriyananda, direct disciple of Paramhansa Yogananda. In 1967, Kriyananda (J. Donald Walters) founded Ananda World Brotherhood Village near Nevada City, California. John is a founding member of this yogic community, which is one of the most successful intentional communities in the world. He is also part of the spiritual directorate led by Kriyananda and, as head of the Ananda Ministry, he offers spiritual guidance to three hundred full-time residents. An inspiring teacher, he has spoken throughout the United States and Europe on spiritual subjects and yogic concepts.

John lives with his wife, Devi, and their son, Mark, in Ananda World Brotherhood Village.

Resources

Author's Suggested Reading List

Autobiography of a Yogi *by Paramhansa Yogananda* A spiritual classic, *Autobiography of a Yogi* describes Yogananda's experiences with great masters of India. It explains with scientific clarity the subtle but definite laws by which yogis perform miracles and attain self-mastery. Available at your local book store. (Published by Self-Realization Fellowship, which is not affiliated with Ananda.)

The following resources are available from Crystal Clarity, Publishers (1-800-424-1055) or at your local bookstore.

The Path: A Spiritual Autobiography *by Kriyananda (J. Donald Walters) The Path* is the moving story of Kriyananda's spiritual awakening and years of training with Paramhansa Yogananda. *The Path* completes Yogananda's life story and includes more than 400 never-before-published stories about him. ***Paperback $6.95***

The Essence of Self Realization: The Wisdom of Paramhansa Yogananda *compiled by Kriyananda (J. Donald Walters)* Nearly 300 sayings and stories that are rich with spiritual wisdom, divine love, and the fullness of spiritual power. Yogananda's conversations are sprinkled with anecdotes; they sparkle with metaphors and contain the deepest insight into all levels of reality. *Paperback $9.95*

Lessons in Yoga: 14 Steps to Higher Awareness *14 Steps to Higher Awareness* is a multidimensional course in meditation and yoga. Each lesson includes sections on meditation, philosophy, yoga postures, breathing, diet, and routine. These lessons, by Kriyananda, go into the science of yoga much more deeply than was possible in this book. Students receive lessons in the mail every other week as well as personal guidance from Ananda's teachers and counselors. Optional tape and video supplements are also available. Call (916) 292-3287 to order these lessons.

Other Resources by Kriyananda

Books:

> *Secrets of Meditation $5.95*
> *Secrets of Inner Peace $5.95*
> *Affirmations for Self-Healing $7.95*
> *Yoga Postures for Higher Awareness $9.95*

Tapes:

> *How to Meditate (six-tape series) $44.95*
> *Meditation: What It Is and How to Do It $9.95*
> *Guided Meditations on the Light $9.95*
> *Metaphysical Meditations $9.95*
> *Yoga Postures for Higher Awareness $9.95*
> *Always Have I Loved Thee (devotional chants written or inspired by Paramhansa Yogananda) $9.95*

Videos:

> *A Course in Meditation (two-video package) $44.95*
> *Yoga Postures for Higher Awareness $24.95*

Ways to Accelerate Your Practice: *The Expanding Light at Ananda World Brotherhood Village* Spending time in a spiritually charged atmosphere with others who meditate is a wonderful way to deepen your meditation practice and your entire spiritual life. Ananda is widely considered to be one of the most successful intentional communities in the world. Ananda's guest facility, *The Expanding Light,* offers a varied, year-round schedule of personal retreats, classes, and special programs. For information call 1-800-346-5350.

Order Form

Crystal Clarity, Publishers specializes in self-help and psychology books. For a complete listing of our products, send for a Crystal Clarity catalogue.

Quantity	Item	Price
————	—————————	———
————	—————————	———
————	—————————	———
————	—————————	———

7.25% Tax in California ———

Shipping & handling charges are based on amount of purchase: Up to $10.00 = $3.00
$10.01 to $20.00 = $4.00
$20.01 to $45.00 = $5.00
$45.01 to $55.00 = $6.00
$55.01 to $65.00 = $7.00
$65.01 to $80.00 = $8.00
Over $80.00 = 10% of total ———

TOTAL ———

Please send payment and order to: Crystal Clarity, 14618 Tyler Foote Road, Nevada City, CA 95959. Call toll-free (800) 424-1055.

Name_____

Address_____

City_____ State ___ Zip _____

Phone_____

Please charge my credit card #_____

☐ VISA ☐ MasterCard Exp. Date_____

Signature _____